GRADES K–2

Using
Benchmark Papers
to Teach Writing
With the Traits

RUTH CULHAM

with Libby Jachles

New York • Toronto • London • Auckland • Sydney
Mexico City • New Delhi • Hong Kong • Buenos Aires

Teaching *Resources*

Cover design by Brian LaRossa
Interior design by Sarah Morrow
Photo on page 5 courtesy of Raymond Coutu
Illustrations on pages 22–24 by Olga and Aleksey Ivanov

Copyright © 2010 by Ruth Culham
All rights reserved. Published by Scholastic Inc.
Printed in the U.S.A.
ISBN-13: 978-0-545-13839-0
ISBN-10: 0-545-13839-6

1 2 3 4 5 6 7 8 9 10   40   16 15 14 13 12 11 10

Contents

Introduction

Since the inception of the writing trait model in the mid-1980s, teachers and students have been better able to communicate about what makes a piece of writing work by focusing discussion on the traits: ideas, organization, voice, word choice, sentence fluency, and conventions. Having a common language for talking about and working with student writing has been a powerful breakthrough in the assessment and teaching of writing. What better way to make the traits concrete than by showing students examples of them in actual writing? Even better, in writing created by students just like themselves?

As teachers have embraced the traits, they have expanded their teaching of writing, moving from simply assigning topics to demonstrating how to make a piece richer in a specific trait. And they have told me—again and again as I travel around the country—how much they need a collection of student work that shows the range of possibilities, from just beginning to strong in every trait.

In response to that need, my colleague Libby Jachles and I have collected hundreds and hundreds of papers during the past several years. We sorted them and selected the exemplars we present in the following pages, a rich and thorough collection of papers that represents the range of written work we've found in kindergarten, first, and second grade.

Specifically, you'll find five papers per trait, ranging from high to low in ideas, organization, voice, word choice, sentence fluency, and conventions, for a total of 30 model papers. Each paper is annotated with a detailed explanation of how it was assessed in that trait, with the remarks correlated to the primary writing scoring guide included in the book. We share a conference comment that we might make to the writer, complimenting him or her on what was done well and posing a suggestion for revision or editing within the specific trait.

Please note that while these papers were selected from primary classes, beginning writers can be found in any grade. You may have students in third, fourth, and even fifth grades and above who will benefit from examining the papers in this collection. Maybe they are new to English, or perhaps writing is a particular challenge for them. No matter the situation, examining how the traits look in beginning writing can help students move ahead in their own writing.

The traits are a powerful way to dig deeply into writing, to show young writers how they are doing and what to try next. The traits provide us with the language to engage young writers in revision and editing, two cornerstones of the writing process. Having a common language for talking about writing makes the whole process easier for kids and teachers alike by helping students understand how writing works. It's never too early to begin teaching students to think and act like writers. They will appreciate having the traits as tools in their ever-growing writer's toolbox.

Part I:
How to Use the Benchmark Paper Collection

From the beginning, samples of student writing have been central to the clarity and validity of the writing traits model. When the traits first emerged in the mid-1980s, teachers gathered samples of student writing and sorted them holistically into piles: high, middle, and low. Those three piles became five as distinctions between papers became more clear: some papers were better than those in the middle, but not quite as good as the ones in the high group, for instance.

Once the papers were sorted, teachers were given the task of documenting why each paper was placed in a specific pile by asking "What makes this paper better or worse than those in adjacent stacks?" Answers were varied: sometimes the idea was not clear, but the spelling and punctuation were strong. In other papers, the sentences were choppy and the words imprecise, yet the introduction and flow of the text worked well. Eventually, the lists of writing qualities that teachers noted were grouped and the traits (ideas, organization, voice, word choice, sentence fluency, and conventions) emerged as six elements found in every sample of writing, no matter how successful the writing might have been overall.

The traits surfaced, were named, and then were defined at different performance levels because teachers closely examined samples of student writing. It's as simple as that. A scoring guide was drafted and used to assess writing. Through this process, an analytic model that pinpointed strengths and revealed weaknesses in each of the six different traits became one of the most valuable tools in the writing teacher's classroom. Once teachers could assess writing with accuracy and reliability, what students needed to improve became crystal clear.

In classrooms across the country and world, teachers use these powerful traits to assess and teach writing in every grade. Although the language in the scoring guides continues to be tightened and clarified, the way the guides are consistently anchored to student writing makes them authentic and powerful tools that will never go out of date.

Defining the Traits for the Beginning Writer

Broken down into six categories, the traits are straightforward and logical. Here is a simple definition of each:

- *Ideas*: the central message of the piece and the details that support it
- *Organization*: the internal structure of the piece
- *Voice*: the tone of the piece—the personal stamp of the writer
- *Word Choice*: the specific vocabulary the writer uses to convey meaning
- *Sentence Fluency*: the way words and phrases flow through the piece
- *Conventions*: the mechanical correctness of the piece

Once you know these traits and begin teaching with them, you will see them stand out in the work of your students. Students will notice them in their own work, paving the way for self-assessment.

Primary students, of course, do not have control over these critical writing skills yet; they are just learning. So, to make the traits more user-friendly for beginning writers, we've broken each one down into four key qualities that are teachable and easy to spot in early writing samples.

Ideas Key Qualities

- Finding a Big Idea
- Focusing on the Big Idea
- Staying With the Big Idea
- Using Juicy Details

Ideas in Beginning Writing

This trait is about the writing's overall message and meaning. It is about the content of the writing. Ideas are strong when they are clear and focused, and move from the general to the specific. Though their texts may not be lengthy, young writers convey ideas by doing the following:

- Drawing pictures with bold lines and lots of color
- Experimenting with letters and words

- Captioning pictures they create themselves and gather from sources
- Talking about what happened to them or their characters
- Asking questions and making lists about things that interest them
- Noticing significance in little things and events

Organization Key Qualities

- Starting with a Bold Beginning
- Developing a Mighty Middle
- Finishing with an Excellent Ending
- Adding a Title

Organization in Beginning Writing

Think of organization as the framework that holds a building together—the concrete foundation, the steel beams, the weight-bearing timbers. When the building is finished, the skeleton isn't visible. What you see instead are the shapes of the rooms, the finished walls, the windows, the light fixtures. But the building is solid because of its sturdy framework. You know it works. Same goes for writing. If you look closely at the work of even emergent writers, you may see signs of organization, such as:

- Several pictures on the same topic, in sequential order
- Information grouped by circling, highlighting, and connecting lines
- A clear beginning and/or ending
- Use of connecting words such as *and, but,* and *so*
- Use of sequencing words such as *first, then, later,* and *the end*
- A sense of time through a sequence of events
- Use of labels, titles, and captions
- Use of lists

Voice Key Qualities

- Expressing a Feeling
- Adding Sparkle and Pizzazz
- Connecting With the Reader
- Saying Things in New Ways

Voice in Beginning Writing

Voice is the writer's passion for the topic coming through loud and clear. It's what keeps us turning the pages of a story long after bedtime. It's what makes an essay about camels fascinating, even though we didn't think we cared all that much about camels. Voice is what primary writers use to assert their own way of looking at an idea. You'll find it in scribbles, in their letter strings, in their sentences, and in their continuous text. Voice can permeate writing, regardless of where the writer falls on the developmental continuum for other traits. Primary writers are well on their way to expressing voice when they exhibit the following:

- Having something important to say
- Creating drawings that are expressive
- Finding new ways of expressing familiar ideas
- Capturing a range of emotions, from gleeful to poignant to afraid
- Offering sincere thoughts
- Confidence that what they say matters
- Demonstration of awareness of an audience
- Willingness to take a risk and try something that no classmate has tried before
- Application of original thinking

Word Choice Key Qualities

- Choosing Verbs That Show Action
- Picking "Just Right" Words
- Reaching for Never-Before-Tried Words
- Using Words to Create Meaning

Word Choice in Beginning Writing

When we explore word choice in the classroom, we focus on the parts of speech that writers use to convey meaning—the nouns, verbs, adjectives, adverbs, pronouns, contractions, gerunds, and so on. These terms may conjure up chilling moments from high school English class, but word choice is not about grammar. It's about selecting words carefully to craft fluent sentences and create a lasting image in the reader's mind. We know that primary students are well on their way to making wise word choices when they do the following:

- Play with letters to make words
- Attempt to write words they have heard

- Try new ways of saying things
- Express an interest in the role of different parts of speech—nouns, verbs, adjectives, and so forth
- Develop a curiosity about language
- Use the perfect word in the perfect place
- Try sensory words
- Use language with precision

Sentence Fluency Key Qualities

- Building Complete Sentences
- Starting Sentences in Different Ways
- Creating Sentences of Different Lengths
- Making Sentences Sound Smooth

Sentence Fluency in Beginning Writing

The sentence fluency trait has two important dimensions: the grammar that makes a group of words a sentence and the way sentences sound. Indeed, this is the auditory trait, where we learn to read with our ears right along with our eyes. Signs that writers are working well with the sentence fluency trait include the following:

- Working with several words in a row, with attention to phrasing
- Being more concerned about sentence quality than sentence correctness
- Experimenting with sentences of varying lengths
- Weaving questions and statements into the text
- Using transitional words to connect one sentence to the next
- Repeating sounds, words, and phrases to create patterns
- Writing passages that can be read aloud with ease

Conventions Key Qualities

- Spacing Words and Sentences
- Using Appropriate Spelling
- Adding Punctuation
- Practicing Capitalization Skills

Conventions in Beginning Writing

Primary writers are too young and inexperienced to show control over sophisticated conventions, but there are certain ones they can follow to make their writing correct and understandable, including the following:

- Imitation and real letters
- Uppercase and lowercase letters
- Conventional spelling of simple words
- Phonetic spelling of both simple and sophisticated words
- End punctuation
- Capital letters at the beginnings of sentences, on proper nouns, and in titles
- *S* for plurals and possessives
- Contractions
- Indented paragraphs

As you assess student writing and share the papers in this book with children, keep in mind the many ways the traits manifest themselves in young writers' work. Writing is an ever-evolving process, and this is never more evident than in the work of beginning writers. As a result, the scoring guides I provide are based on a developmental continuum, documenting the steps and stages writing goes through on its way to getting strong and standing on its own. Moments of brilliance may show themselves in pictures, for instance, long before the writer can capture the same idea with voice and use an extended vocabulary. Each child progresses differently; some move forward quickly, while others need more time and support to develop as writers. But make no mistake about it: regardless of skill and experience, students improve when they are shown what they are doing well and specifically how to improve. The traits are the underpinnings of successful writing that emerge as students develop as writers.

Noticing what young writers do, naming it, and showing them the next steps to take are critical to their success. Good writing happens over time and with lots of practice and lots of support. The traits give you the language and structure to move students along the writing continuum from Ready to Begin to Established.

Understanding and Using the Beginning Writer's Scoring Guides

The trait scoring guides on pages 14–19 allow you to assess student writing and provide feedback that students can use to make their current and future work stronger. Scores range from 1 to 5 in each of the traits. For example, if a student writes the roughest of drafts, showing little control and skill in the trait that you're assessing, he or she would receive a score of 1, Ready to Begin. But if his or her piece shows strong control and skill in the trait, he or she would receive a score of 5, Established.

This book provides an exemplar for each point along the scale for each trait along with an explanation of the score and a suggested comment to share with the student during a conference.

Scoring Guide: **Ideas**

The central message of the piece and the details that support it

score 5 Established

A. The idea is clear and coherent.

B. The text is a well-developed paragraph.

C. Elaboration through interesting details creates meaning for the reader.

D. The writer shows understanding of the topic through personal experience or research.

E. Pictures (if present) enhance the key ideas but aren't necessary for comprehension.

score 4 Extending

A. The writing works by itself to explain a simple idea or story.

B. The writing is made up of several sentences on one topic.

C. Key details begin to surface.

D. The writing makes sense, but some information may be missing or irrelevant.

E. Pictures and text work harmoniously to create a rich treatment of the topic.

score 3 Expanding

A. The idea is written in a basic sentence.

B. A simple statement with somewhat detailed pictures captures the topic.

C. Basic details are present in the text; the illustrations work to enhance the main idea.

D. The text contains words, but no sentences.

E. Text and pictures are understandable to the reader.

score 2 Exploring

A. One or more ideas are present in the most general way.

B. Letters and words can be picked out as clues to the topic.

C. The drawing helps to clarify the idea.

D. The text is composed of simple, recognizable letters with some early attempts at words.

E. The reader gets the basic idea but needs the writer's assistance to comprehend it fully.

score 1 Ready to Begin

A. The piece conveys little meaning.

B. Real-life objects show up in drawings.

C. Drawings may not be completely recognizable.

D. Letters are not consistent or standard.

E. An oral reading by the writer is needed to understand the message.

Scoring Guide: **Organization**

The internal structure of the piece

score 5

Established

A. The title (if present) is thoughtful and effective.

B. There is a clear beginning, middle, and end.

C. Important ideas are highlighted within the text.

D. Everything fits together nicely.

E. The text slows down and speeds up to highlight the ideas and show the writer's skill at pacing.

F. Clear transitions connect one sentence to the next.

score 4

Extending

A. The title (if present) comes close to capturing the central idea.

B. The writing starts out strong but ends predictably.

C. The writer uses a pattern to spotlight the most important details.

D. Ideas follow a logical but obvious sequence.

E. The pace of the writing is even; it doesn't bog the reader down.

F. Basic transitions link one sentence to the next.

score 3

Expanding

A. The simple title (if present) conveys the topic.

B. The piece contains a beginning but not a conclusion.

C. The piece is little more than a list of sentences connected by theme.

D. There is basic order with a few missteps.

E. There is more text at the beginning than in the middle or end.

F. Sentence parts are linked with conjunctions (*but, and, or*).

score 2

Exploring

A. The piece has no title.

B. Letters or words are used as captions.

C. Simple clues about order emerge in pictures or text.

D. The arrangement of pictures or text shows an awareness of the importance of structure and pattern.

E. Left-to-right, top-to-bottom orientation is evident.

F. No transitions are used.

score 1

Ready to Begin

A. Letters (if present) are scattered across the page.

B. No coordination of written elements is evident.

C. Lines, pictures, or letters are randomly placed on the page.

D. Lines, pictures, or letters are grouped haphazardly.

E. There is no sense of order.

Scoring Guide: **Voice**

The tone of the piece—the personal stamp of the writer

score 5
Established

A. The writer "owns" the topic.

B. The piece contains the writer's imprint.

C. The writer is mindful of his or her audience and connects purposefully to the reader.

D. The tone is identifiable—bittersweet, compassionate, frustrated, terrified, and so on.

E. The writer takes real risks, creating a truly individual piece of writing.

score 4
Extending

A. The writer takes a standard topic and addresses it in a nonstandard way.

B. The writer tries a new word, interesting image, or unusual detail.

C. The piece speaks to the reader in several places.

D. The writing captures a general mood such as happy, sad, or mad.

E. The writer begins to show how he or she thinks and feels about the topic.

score 3
Expanding

A. There are fleeting glimpses of the writer's perspective on the topic.

B. The text and pictures contain touches of originality.

C. There is a moment of audience awareness, but then it fades.

D. Oversize letters, exclamation points, underlining, repetition, and pictures are used for emphasis.

E. A pat summary statement conceals the writer's individuality.

score 2
Exploring

A. The piece is a routine response to the assignment.

B. The piece is made up of environmental text and only a bit of original text.

C. The text connects with the reader in the most general way.

D. The drawings begin to reveal the individual.

E. The barest hint of the writer is evident.

score 1
Ready to Begin

A. The reader is not sure why the writer chose this idea for writing.

B. The writer copies what he or she sees displayed around the room.

C. No awareness of audience is evident.

D. The piece contains very simple drawings or lines.

E. Nothing distinguishes the work to make it the writer's own.

Ready
to move to
the grades
3–5
scoring
guide!

Scoring Guide: **Word Choice**

The specific vocabulary the writer uses to convey meaning

score 5 Established

A. The writer uses everyday words and phrases with a fresh and original spin.

B. The words paint a clear picture in the reader's mind.

C. The writer uses just the right words or phrases.

D. The piece contains good use of figurative language.

E. Words are used correctly, colorfully, and with creativity.

score 4 Extending

A. Proper nouns (e.g., *Raisin Bran*) are combined with standard ones (e.g., *cereal*).

B. The writer uses an active verb or two.

C. There is very little repetition of words.

D. The writer attempts figurative language.

E. The writer "stretches" by using different types of words.

score 3 Expanding

A. Some words make sense.

B. The reader begins to see what the writer is describing.

C. One or two words stand out.

D. Occasional misuse of words bogs the reader down.

E. The writer tries out new words.

score 2 Exploring

A. Conventional letters are present.

B. The letter strings begin to form words.

C. Letter strings can be read as words even though the spacing and spelling aren't correct.

D. Words from the board, displays, or word walls are attempted.

E. A few words can be identified.

score 1 Ready to Begin

A. The page contains scribbles and random lines.

B. Imitation letters may be present.

C. There may be random strings of letters across the page.

D. Writer uses his or her name.

E. Few, if any, recognizable words are present.

Scoring Guide: **Sentence Fluency**

The way words and phrases flow through the piece

score 5 Established

A. Different sentence lengths give the writing a nice sound. There is playfulness and experimentation.

B. Varied sentence beginnings create a pleasing rhythm.

C. Different kinds of sentences (statements, commands, questions, and exclamations) are present.

D. The flow from one sentence to the next is smooth.

E. The piece is a breeze to read aloud.

score 4 Extending

A. Sentences are of different lengths.

B. Sentences start differently.

C. Some sentences read smoothly, while others still need work.

D. Conjunctions are correctly used in long and short sentences.

E. Aside from a couple of awkward moments, the piece can be read aloud easily.

score 3 Expanding

A. Simple sentences contain basic subject-verb agreement (e.g., "I jump.").

B. Sentence beginnings are structured identically, making all sentences sound alike.

C. Longer sentences go on and on.

D. Simple conjunctions, such as *and* and *but*, are used to make compound sentences.

E. The piece is easy to read aloud, although it may contain repetitive or awkward sentence patterns.

score 2 Exploring

A. Words and punctuation marks work together in units.

B. The piece contains many short, repetitive phrases.

C. Awkward language patterns break the flow of the piece.

D. The reader gets only one or two clues about the connection between pictures and text.

E. The writer stumbles when reading the text aloud and may have to back up and reread.

score 1 Ready to Begin

A. It's hard to figure out connections between text elements.

B. Words, if present, stand alone.

C. Imitation words and letters are used across the page.

D. There is no overall sense of flow to the piece.

E. Only the writer can read the piece aloud.

Scoring Guide: **Conventions**

The mechanical correctness of the piece

score 5 — Established

A. High-use words are spelled correctly and others are easy to read.

B. The writer applies basic capitalization rules with consistency.

C. Punctuation marks are used effectively to guide the reader.

D. One or more indented paragraphs are present.

E. Standard English grammar is used.

F. Conventions are applied consistently and accurately.

score 4 — Extending

A. Spelling is correct or close on high-use words (e.g., *kiten, saed, wint*).

B. Sentence beginnings and proper nouns are usually capitalized.

C. The writer uses end punctuation and series commas correctly.

D. The writer may try more advanced punctuation (dashes, ellipses, quotation marks), but not always with success.

E. Only minor editing is required to show thoughtful use of conventions.

score 3 — Expanding

A. Spelling is inconsistent but readable (phonetic spelling, such as kitn, sed, wnt).

B. Uppercase and lowercase letters are used correctly.

C. Capitals mark the beginning of sentences.

D. End-punctuation marks are generally used correctly.

E. The writer follows simple conventions correctly.

score 2 — Exploring

A. The words are unreadable to the untrained eye (quasi-phonetic spelling, such as KN, sD, Wt).

B. There is little discrimination between uppercase and lowercase letters.

C. Spacing between letters and words is present.

D. The writer experiments with punctuation.

E. The use of conventions is not consistent.

score 1 — Ready to Begin

A. Letters are written in strings (pre-phonetic spelling, such as gGmkrRt).

B. Letters are formed irregularly; there is no intentional use of uppercase and lowercase letters.

C. Spacing is uneven between letters and words.

D. Punctuation is not present.

E. The piece does not contain standard conventions.

Honing Assessment Skills Using the Benchmark Papers

There is no single better way to get a handle on the traits than to use the scoring guide to assess student writing. Repeated practice with the scoring guide creates familiarity with each trait. It helps focus your evaluation on the key qualities of a trait, offering a way into the writing so you can figure out what is working as well as what still needs attention.

And that is where instruction needs to start—where the student needs it, as demonstrated by assessment. However, over the years of working with the traits, I've noticed that the first thing many teachers do is head straight for the lessons or the picture books, enjoying sharing ideas and books and adding a new spin by including references to the traits. Many teachers report that using literature to teach writing has been very successful; it motivates students and inspires them to write. But, we have to ask ourselves: Does teaching the traits randomly, without a focus or purpose, maximize improvement in writing? In my long experience, I have seen the most marked improvement when teachers rely on assessment to guide their instruction, using the traits as a tool for talking about writing, making concepts explicit, and making writing manageable for students.

But, sadly, many teachers feel inadequately prepared to use the traits where they are the most powerful—in assessment. Assessment is how we sort out what students know and what confuses them. So it's best to begin right here, in the power zone. How else will you know, with confidence, that time spent teaching a lesson or sharing a book that focuses on a specific trait is what your students need most to improve? First you assess, then you identify the key qualities of the traits that small groups or the whole class have yet to master, and then you plan a lesson that addresses the most urgent need.

The student papers in this book have been scored and annotated so you can practice assessing. Trust me—to get really good at teaching writing using the traits, you must be adept at spotting key qualities in student writing. The way to develop this skill with the traits is to sit down for an hour or two of quiet, uninterrupted time, read each piece, match it to the assessment provided, and analyze the scores and comments. You'll be surprised at how quickly it goes once you get started. And the result is an insider's perspective on the writing of your students—the most valuable tool in your teaching arsenal.

To get started, simply follow these guidelines:

1. Choose a trait and read all five papers in that section.

2. Assess one of the papers using the scoring guide that appears on pages 14–19.

3. Read the scoring guides' descriptors for each of the five levels, from top— 5: Established, to bottom—1: Ready to Begin.

4. Assign a score of 1, 2, 3, 4, or 5 to the trait and write it on the paper or on a separate page you keep for practice scoring.

5. Compare your score to the one provided in this book. Read the explanation of how it was scored and see whether we agree. Do your students exhibit many of the same writing characteristics as the writers of these papers?

6. Notice the comment at the end of each assessed paper. Primary students benefit most from our comments to them and our gentle nudges forward. These comments are provided to give you ideas for how to use the language of the traits to both validate what has been accomplished and propel students to new writing territory.

7. Read the other papers in the same trait and score them using the same process.

8. Choose a second trait and continue until you've had practice in all six and feel confident.

9. If you want additional guided practice, use the papers in *6+1 Traits: The Complete Guide for the Primary Grades*. Each trait chapter contains five additional papers for you to practice assessing, with explanations for how each paper was scored.

Once you've assessed the papers in this book, you'll be ready to share them with students.

Student-Friendly Scoring Guides

The origin of the six-trait model stems from the work of teachers examining student writing and describing what works and what needs work using consistent language: the traits. Teachers who go through this process are the ones who understand the fundamentals of good writing and how to spot it in the work of their students. So it only makes sense that as soon as possible, young writers should examine writing through the lens of the traits as well, developing a keen understanding of what good writing looks like and how to create it for many different purposes. It not only makes sense—it works!

We've also included two versions of student-friendly scoring guides for primary writers. In the first version (pages 22–24), for the youngest writers who are still developing their reading skills, pictures provide the context to begin discussions about each trait and what writers hope to achieve. The second set of student-friendly guides (pages 25–27) can be used by the end of first grade and into second as students become more skilled readers. They will appreciate having a simplified version to refer to as they write, revise, and edit.

A Wise Owl Knows Everything About Her Idea

Just Starting   **On My Way**   **I've Got It!**

ORGANIZATION

A Well-Organized Squirrel is Ready for Winter

Just Starting   **On My Way**   **I've Got It!**

A Lion's Proud Voice Rules the Pride

Just Starting   **On My Way**   **I've Got It!**

A Monkey Uses Word Choice to Chatter in the Jungle

Just Starting   **On My Way**   **I've Got It!**

A Snake Slithers Smoothly Like a Sentence Across the Desert Floor

Just Starting　　　　**On My Way**　　　　**I've Got It!**

A Raccoon Cleans Up His Conventions Before He Eats

Just Starting　　　　**On My Way**　　　　**I've Got It!**

My First Scoring Guide
Organization

Strong — **I've Got It!**
* I have a bold beginning, mighty middle, and excellent ending.
* My details are in the right places.
* I've given my ideas an order that really works.

Developing — **On My Way**
* I've made a good start at a beginning, middle, and ending.
* Most of my details fit.
* The order of my ideas makes sense.

Beginning — **Just Beginning**
* My writing doesn't have a clear beginning, middle, or ending.
* My details are jumbled and confusing.
* I have "stuff" on paper, but it's not in order.

My First Scoring Guide
Ideas

Strong — **I've Got it!**
* I know A LOT about this topic.
* My writing is bursting with fascinating details.
* I've picked a topic small enough to handle.

Developing — **On My Way**
* I know enough to get a good start.
* Some of my details are too general.
* My topic might be a little too big.

Beginning — **Just Beginning**
* I haven't figured out what to say.
* The details aren't clear.
* I'm still thinking and looking for a topic.

My First Scoring Guide
Word Choice

Strong

I've Got It!

* I've picked exactly the right words.
* My words are colorful, fresh, and snappy.
* The words help my reader see my ideas.

Developing

On My Way

* Some of my words work well, but others don't.
* I've used too many ordinary words.
* My words paint a general picture of the idea.

Beginning

Just Beginning

* I'm confused about how to use words well.
* I've left out key words.
* Many of my words are the same or just wrong.

My First Scoring Guide
Voice

Strong

I've Got It!

* My writing sounds like me.
* The reader will know I care about this topic.
* I have the right amount of energy in this piece.

Developing

On My Way

* My writing is safe. You only get a glimpse of me.
* I have only a passing interest in this topic.
* My energy level is uneven in this piece.

Beginning

Just Beginning

* I forgot to add what I think and feel in this piece.
* I really don't care at all about this topic.
* I'm bored and it shows.

My First Scoring Guide
Conventions

I've Got It! — Strong

* My spelling is magnificent.
* All my capitals are in the right places.
* I used punctuation correctly to make my writing easy to read.
* I've used correct grammar and added paragraphs where needed.
* I've done a great job proofreading.

On My Way — Developing

* Only my simpler words are spelled correctly.
* I've used capitals in easy spots.
* I have correct punctuation in some places, but not in others.
* I proofread quickly and missed some things.

Just Beginning — Beginning

* It's hard to read my words because of the spelling.
* My capitals don't follow the rules.
* I haven't used punctuation well at all.
* I forgot to proofread.

My First Scoring Guide
Sentence Fluency

I've Got It! — Strong

* My sentences are well-built and easy to read aloud.
* The way my sentences begin makes them interesting.
* I've varied my sentence lengths.

On My Way — Developing

* I've got sentences! Some of them are hard to read aloud, though.
* I've tried a couple of different ways to begin my sentences.
* I might put some sentences together or I could cut a few in two.

Just Beginning — Beginning

* I am having trouble making a sentence.
* My beginnings all sound the same.
* I've used *and* too many times or many sentences are too short.

Teaching Writing With Benchmark Papers

We've seen that assessing papers can deepen your understanding of the traits and help you identify what a writer is ready to learn next. In the same way, reading and discussing sample papers can help students grasp a key quality and see what the next step in their own writing might look like. This section shares several ways you can use the benchmark papers as teaching tools in your classroom.

Teaching with benchmark papers is most effective when all students can see the papers under discussion. Of course, you can always make copies for the group you're working with or the entire class. But the technology found in most classrooms offers exciting alternatives to the dreary copy machine. With the accompanying CD and an electronic projection system, you can project the papers in this book for students so you and your class can enjoy reading the papers and noticing how the traits show themselves in each.

All papers are included as PDFs. In addition, I have selected one high and one low paper for each trait to be explored in depth and have created interactive PDFs to guide student discussion. With these PDFs, you can click on a key quality and examine how it was handled in a particular paper.

This is a dream come true for many teachers because we have yearned to show students in lively, engaging ways what makes good writing work. It's also useful to show students exactly why some papers are scored lower and what to do to make them stronger. For more detailed information on how to use the interactive PDFs, please see the guidelines on page 96.

I hope the lessons that follow spark ideas for using the papers in whole-group, small-group, and one-on-one settings.

A Model Lesson for Large-Group Instruction

Target Trait: Word Choice

Paper #1: "Playdrama"

Lesson Focus: Students will read and assess a sample paper for the word choice trait. They will brainstorm new words that would improve the writing and make a list of strong and interesting words to include in the writing of their own.

Materials Needed

- Student paper to project from CD
- Student-friendly guide for word choice (one of two versions provided)

- Student writing journals or notebooks
- Pencils, crayons, markers

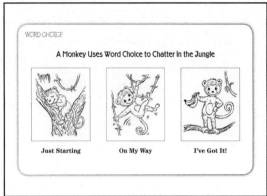

What to Do

1. Gather the students on the rug in front of the interactive whiteboard and project the paper. Give students time to examine the pictures and read the text aloud as they follow along.

2. Explain to students that when writers work, they use words right along with pictures to help communicate what they want to say. Say, "When we talk about the words a writer uses, that's the word choice trait." Highlight the words *word choice* on the screen.

3. Ask students if they can tell what this writer was trying to show in his or her pictures and text. (Students may likely respond that it looks like there are people, perhaps friends, playing and going somewhere in a car or other vehicle. They may not recognize the word *play* in the writing, but you most likely will.)

4. Ask, "Can you tell what words the writer is using to tell the story?" Highlight the first picture and letter string. (Students may comment that the first picture and the letter string seem to be about playing.)

5. Hand out one of the student-friendly guides for the word choice trait. Ask students to assess the writing and discuss their response with a partner. Invite volunteer pairs to share their assessments and their reasons. (Students will likely find the piece to be "Just Starting.")

6. Explain that the writing the students are looking at is by a student who is just beginning to use words. Point out the words you notice the student trying in the text if students don't spot them on their own.

7. Ask students to think of other words they could add to the piece to explain more about what is happening. Brainstorm the words and make a list on the side of the whiteboard.

8. Ask students to choose two or three words they like best to go with the sample writing. Show students how to insert the words into the original text. Encourage students to keep brainstorming as many interesting words as they can think of for the first and second pictures, writing them down as they call them out.

9. After they have finished, tell students that their word choice has improved the piece a great deal and discuss why. Refer them to their student-friendly guide and ask where the piece might score now that it has been revised for word choice.

10. Ask students to think about other words they might add if time allows. Congratulate students for their good word choice work and send them back to their desks or tables.

11. Have students take out their writing notebooks and select a piece that they think needs work in the word choice trait.

12. Ask students to brainstorm working with a partner, at least five new words they could use to make the writing more interesting. Tell them to write those words on the same page as their draft so they don't forget them if they want to revise later. Encourage students to write the best words they can think of and not to be hindered by the spelling, which can be corrected later.

13. Ask volunteers to share their new words. Tell students they can use any of the words their classmates shared in their own writing. Writers borrow words from each other all the time.

14. Remind students that using good word choice means writing words that they like, that make pictures in the reader's mind, and that explain what they are thinking.

A Model Lesson for Small-Group Instruction

Target Trait: Organization

Paper #5: "A Scary Story"

Lesson Focus: Working with a small group of students who are learning how to put events in order, students will read a narrative paper strong in organization and discuss how the events unfold. They will examine the paper for time words or sequence and transition clues. Then they will apply what they learn about organization to a piece of their own writing.

Materials Needed

- Student paper to project from CD
- Student-friendly guide for organization (one of two versions provided)
- Student writing journals or notebooks
- Pencils, crayons, markers

What to Do

1. Gather a small group of students around the whiteboard. Ask them to bring a piece of their writing, a pencil, and their student-friendly guide for word choice.

2. Ask students to tell you what comes to mind when you say "organization." (Students may respond with things they need to organize, such as their rooms, their desks, and so on.) Remind them that writers need to be organized when they tell stories, too. The events have to be in order from beginning to end if the reader is to understand what happens.

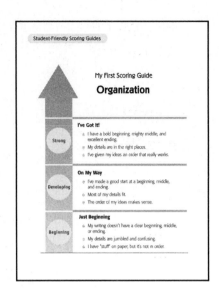

3. Project the paper and read it aloud with the students.

4. Ask students if they think the details of the story were organized in an effective way. (They should respond positively to this piece.)

5. Ask students to review their student-friendly guides, then tell you which pictures or wording (depending on the guide you are using) explains why the projected piece is strong in organization.

6. Tell students that writers give the readers clues to show how information in the writing is connected by using sequence words or transition statements.

7. Highlight the organization words and phrases on the paper: phrases and words should turn color.

8. Ask students to tell you which phrases help the organization of the piece. (*Once upon a time, every night, one night, next, last,* and so on.)

9. Brainstorm one more event that could be added to the story. (Then, he spooked some kids on their way to school; then, he spooked a dog that was out for a walk; and so on.) Ask them to tell you the event first. Settle on one the group likes in particular, and see which time or sequence word they'd like to use to show how it fits in the story, such as *then, next,* or *another time.*

10. Ask a volunteer to add the sentence to the whiteboard. Show him or her how to use the symbol to show where the sentence should be inserted into the story. Explain that writers use this symbol so they don't have to rewrite their whole paper when revising.

11. Encourage other students to think of more lines that could be added, but make sure each begins with a sequence word to show time or order.

12. Ask students to return to their seats and look through their journals or notebooks for a piece of writing that they can revise for organization. Tell them to add key time or order words in places if they were not there on the first draft. Remind them to use the caret symbol (∧) to insert a new word or short phrases so they don't have to rewrite their whole sentence or story.

13. Ask students to discuss the trait of organization and why it is important for writers to leave clues for readers about how ideas connect, relate, or occur

in sequence. Tell them to keep their eyes out for new sequence words or phrases they find as they read that can be used to make their own writing well organized.

A Model Lesson for One-on-One Conferring

Target Trait: Ideas

Paper #3: "My Spahl tng"

Lesson Focus: In an individual conference, a student will learn to transform a general idea, such as the one in this example piece, to one that is more specific and has more details. Once the model paper has been revised, the student will apply the same technique to a piece of his or her own writing that needs improvement in the ideas trait.

Materials Needed

- Student paper to project from CD
- Student-friendly guide for ideas (one of two versions provided)
- A piece of the student's writing
- Pencils, crayons, markers

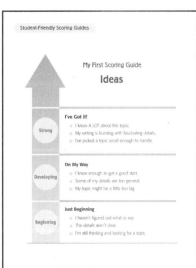

What to Do

1. Ask a student to join you at the whiteboard and bring a piece of writing he or she is working on, the student-friendly guide for the ideas trait, and a pencil.

2. Show the student the sample paper for the ideas trait and read it aloud as he or she follows along.

3. Ask the student to tell you what this piece was about. (The response will likely include information that the writer wrote about his or her dad and how much he or she misses him.)

4. Display the student-friendly guide for the ideas trait next to the sample writing on the whiteboard. Ask the student to think about how strong the idea is in the model paper and if it could be revised to be even clearer. (The piece receives a "3" in the ideas trait, about halfway there.)

5. Tell the student that readers sometimes have questions when they read if the writer hasn't added enough details. Ask the student whether he or she has any questions for the writer about this piece. Write the questions under the student writing sample as the student shares them. (Questions such as: What did you do with your dad that was fun? What is something about your dad that is special? Where did your dad go? What else is in the picture with your dad?)

6. Ask the student to pick his or her favorite question, and talk together about what the answer might be. If, for example, the student chooses, "What is something about your dad that is special?" you might brainstorm that when he laughs, he snorts. Or, that when it's time for bed, the dad always reads a really good book to the son or daughter and uses great voices for all the characters.

7. Depending on what is decided, show the student where the detail might go in the writing. Let the student add the detail to the sample piece of writing.

8. Ask the student to share his or her piece of writing with you by reading it aloud. Tell the student you will listen carefully and think of one question that could add to the idea.

9. Allow time for the student to read. Then ask the student one question about some part of the idea that could use more information or detail to be clearer.

10. Ask the student to tell you his or her answer. Then ask what could be added to the writing to include that detail or piece of information.

11. Give the student time to add to the piece. Ask the student to reread the piece to you, and ask if it has improved in the ideas trait.

12. Ask him or her to think of one more detail that could be added. Brainstorm other questions to be answered if he or she has trouble coming up with an idea. Encourage the student to add more details and develop the piece as much as possible. Remember that pictures can also develop a piece if the writer's written vocabulary is not extensive.

Help! I Don't Have an Interactive Whiteboard!

Don't panic. Although you may not have the technology to highlight a trait within each paper electronically, you can still use these papers to practice assessing and to help students understand the traits as well.

Project the papers on an Elmo or an overhead projector. If you wish, you can make a copy of the paper you want students to read and discuss, then give them highlighters to mark key passages. You are still using student writing to teach what a trait is and how it works. If the latest technology is still not on the horizon for you and your class, do the lessons the old-fashioned way! They will work just as well.

Extending the Collection

Once you've practiced assessing and are comfortable using the scoring guide, you'll enjoy collecting samples of student work that come from your own classroom, school, or district. The samples in this book are from everywhere—every state has contributed in one way or another. However, teachers often indicate they'd like to have more papers from their local population. It takes time and a little organization to make this happen, but you can do it and will undoubtedly appreciate the results for years to come.

If you and your colleagues want to start your own collection of anchor papers, I recommend collecting about 200 papers per grade level as you begin. Set aside the time to read and sort the papers, putting sticky notes on ones that strike you as excellent examples of a trait at each of the different performance levels. You'll move papers around from trait to trait until you have the right number, and you may find you need even more papers to choose from before you are finished.

Here are some tips for collecting and sorting:

1. Have more papers on hand than you think you could possibly use. You'll be surprised how many it takes to find the "just right" examples for each point on the scale for each trait.

2. Consider having more than one anchor paper for each point along the scale. Expand your paper collection to include narrative, expository, and persuasive writing to show examples of different purposes for writing.

3. Provide short annotations explaining the score for each paper.

4. Post the papers on a school or district Web site for all teachers to use and enjoy. Invite collaboration and include new papers every year. Be sure to get parent permission with a district- or school-approved student release form if you publish the papers in any format, paper or electronic.

Part II:
The Benchmark Papers

The following 30 student papers have been scored for each trait, and an annotation is included to explain how it was scored as an anchor paper for a particular trait. Have fun with these papers! You'll enjoy assessing them to become a consistent and reliable rater, and it will be even more delightful sharing them with your students.

Analysis of the Ideas Trait in "The Wrene"

What We See in the Writing

This child most likely has a good sense of story. The drawings seem to indicate that the writer has listened to many fairy tales. Without an interpretation, it's impossible to tell what the message of this writing is. The scoring guide descriptors for level 1, Ready to Begin, match this writer's performance.

A. *The piece conveys little meaning.*

While this piece contains both writing and a somewhat detailed picture, the meaning is not clear.

B. *Real-life objects show up in drawings.*

The drawings show a building of sorts and a person. The writer has the start of a good idea; we just don't know what that idea is yet.

C. *Drawings may not be completely recognizable.*

The drawings themselves are recognizable. Details such as the hat, the extension of the legs, and the height of the building create confusion.

D. *Letters are not consistent or standard.*

Though the letters start out with some consistency, they soon fade into more of a scribble.

E. *An oral reading by the writer is needed to understand the message.*

The writer's help is needed in order to allow the reader to clearly understand the message.

What We Say to the Writer

Where did you get your idea for this story? There are so many details in your picture. Can you tell me more about the character and the setting that you've drawn? I'm going to write down on a sticky note some of the words you use to describe them so that you can use them in your writing.

Scoring Guide

The paper rated these scores on a 5-point scale.

IDEAS	**1**
Organization	2
Voice	2
Word Choice	2
Sentence Fluency	1
Conventions	1

Ideas

Organization

Voice

Word Choice

Sentence Fluency

Conventions

Analysis of the Ideas Trait in "I No Wut Lady Bug like"

What We See in the Writing

This writer probably spends a fair amount of time outdoors, observing things in nature. The text, "I NO Wut Lad BuG like," is supported by a picture, but stops short of telling the reader what ladybugs like. The descriptors at level 2, Exploring, match this student's writing performance.

A. One or more ideas are present in the most general way.

A single sentence accompanies the picture of a ladybug and a flower. It's a powerful, intriguing sentence that connects with the reader to add voice, but it's still only one sentence.

> ## Scoring Guide
> *The paper rated these scores on a 5-point scale.*
>
> | | |
> |---|---|
> | **IDEAS** | **2** |
> | Organization | 4 |
> | Voice | 4 |
> | Word Choice | 3 |
> | Sentence Fluency | 4 |
> | Conventions | 2 |

B. Letters and words can be picked out as clues to the topic.

Letters and words clearly convey that this writer knows what ladybugs like. A fascinating invitation to tell us more. Unfortunately, the writer does not continue to tell us what that is.

C. The drawing helps to clarify the idea.

While the words "Lad BuG" are easy to pick out as *ladybug*, the picture really seals the deal. The reader might also infer from the picture that ladybugs like flowers.

D. The text is composed of simple, recognizable letters with some early attempts at words.

"NO" for *know*, "Wut" for *what*, "Lad BuG" for *ladybug*, are excellent attempts at words. This writer is not afraid to take a risk.

E. The reader gets the basic idea but needs the writer's assistance to comprehend it fully.

The picture and text are quite clear. A chat with the writer would clarify the unwritten part of this piece—what ladybugs like.

What We Say to the Writer

I can tell that you spend time outside observing things in nature. Your picture has many details, and the colors make it very clear. When you wrote that you know what ladybugs like, you really made me curious! I see that you've drawn a flower. Is that what ladybugs like? I'll write that word on a sticky note so that you can add it to your writing.

Ideas

Organization

Voice

Word Choice

Sentence Fluency

Conventions

I NO WUt LaD BUG liKe.

Analysis of the Ideas Trait in "My Spahl tng"

What We See in the Writing

The picture and writing clearly tell the reader that this young writer cherishes a picture of her dad. Three complete sentences stay on topic. This piece scores at level 3, Expanding, for the trait of ideas.

A. *The idea is written in a basic sentence.*

"My SPAHL tNg si a PIKR ov MY DAD. I miss my DAD. I lovo my DAD." The idea of this writing is very clear and written in basic sentences.

B. *A simple statement with somewhat detailed pictures captures the topic.*

Three simple sentences and a picture of only Dad let the reader know what's important to this little one. Picture and text are on topic.

> ## Scoring Guide
> *The paper rated these scores on a 5-point scale.*
>
> | | |
> |---|---|
> | **IDEAS** | **3** |
> | Organization | 3 |
> | Voice | 3 |
> | Word Choice | 3 |
> | Sentence Fluency | 3 |
> | Conventions | 2 |

C. *Basic details are present in the text; the illustrations work to enhance the main idea.*

The text clearly states that a picture of Dad is the writer's special thing. The details in the drawing of Dad deepen the reader's understanding of this and suggest he or she spends time looking closely at this photo.

D. *The text contains words, but no sentences.*

"My," "a," Dad," "miss" are spelled correctly. While some of the other words are a stretch ("SPAHL" for *special*, "PIKR" for *picture*), the experienced reader read the words in these basic sentences.

E. *Text and pictures are understandable to the reader.*

The text and picture are easily understandable to the reader. The writer elaborates on her special picture, saying she misses her dad and loves her dad.

What We Say to the Writer

I can tell that your dad's picture is very important to you. Where do you keep his picture? When you say that you miss your dad, it makes me wonder where he is. I think other readers will want to know these details, too.

MY SPAiL tN9 si a PfKR ov MY DA0. T miss MY DA0. F 1010 MY DA0.

Analysis of the Ideas Trait in "the Sun is a stre"

What We See in the Writing

This young writer has included multiple sentences on one topic, with an illustration to match the text. Sentences are simple but show that the student has much information on the topic. The descriptors for level 4, Extending, match this text.

Scoring Guide

The paper rated these scores on a 5-point scale.

IDEAS	**4**
Organization	4
Voice	3
Word Choice	4
Sentence Fluency	4
Conventions	3

A. *The writing works by itself to explain a simple idea or story.*

Even without the illustration, this writing conveys much information about the sun and the stars.

B. *The writing is made up of several sentences on one topic.*

Five sentences provide plenty of information about the sun.

C. *Key details begin to surface.*

Clearly, this writer is interested in what she's learned about the sun. It is the hottest star, there are other stars around it, and planets go around the sun.

D. *The writing makes sense, but some information may be missing or irrelevant.*

This writing is clear, on topic, and makes sense. As this writer learns more, it wouldn't be surprising to see future pieces on this topic.

E. *Pictures and text work harmoniously to create a rich treatment of the topic.*

The picture shows the sun, with other stars around it, and a planet (Earth) going around the sun. Pictures and text match beautifully.

What We Say to the Writer

You know so much about the sun. Thanks for writing about this. Your writing is so clear, and your readers will be able to learn from the information you share. Is there more you want to know about the sun, or stars, or planets? I can't wait to see what else you write about.

the Sun is a stre. It $ the hots stre Ih the wrlde. The sun has stre a rohd it. thra aswe the str that you see at night. The plani go a rohd the sun.

Analysis of the Ideas Trait in "I'm a blond yellow cat"

What We See in the Writing

Do you want to know what makes cats tick? Just ask this writer. The sentences elaborate on what makes this cat happy and what makes her mad. The writing is clear and confident. This piece scores a 5, Established, for the trait of ideas.

Scoring Guide

The paper rated these scores on a 5-point scale.

IDEAS	**5**
Organization	5
Voice	5
Word Choice	5
Sentence Fluency	5
Conventions	5

A. The idea is clear and coherent.

This piece provides a clear idea of some of the details in the life of a blond yellow cat.

B. The text is a well-developed paragraph.

From start to finish, this writing stays on topic. Four sentences provide the reader with a glimpse of the cat's clever personality.

C. Elaboration through interesting details creates meaning for the reader.

Can't you just picture this? The blond yellow cat rubs against a chair leg. Give the cat "tunna," and she'll purr. Don't, and you'd better watch out!

D. The writer shows understanding of the topic through personal experience or research.

It's quite evident that this writer has a cat in her family. No question, either, that this cat loves "tunna" . . . and knows how to get it. Personal experience helps the writer know just what makes a cat tick (or purr, as the case may be).

E. Pictures (if present) enhance the key ideas but aren't necessary for comprehension.

While the detailed picture enhances the story, it isn't needed to understand the writer's message.

What We Say to the Writer

I love the way you wrote this from the cat's point of view. How did you come up with such a clever idea? You know a lot about cats. Do you have one? I have a feeling there may be more stories about this cat in the future. Do you think you'll write more about her interesting adventures?

I'm a blond yellow cat. I rub
up against a chair leg untill
I get tunna. I look around
for happynes and when I see
it I purr. When I get mad I
hiss like a sneaey snake.

Analysis of the Organization Trait in "B"

What We See in the Writing

Looking at this piece, it's hard to decipher the writing or the picture. There is no sense of order. The scoring guide descriptors for level 1, Ready to Begin, match this writer's performance.

A. *Letters (if present) are scattered across the page.*

There are some random letters on the page.

B. *No coordination of written elements is evident.*

It's possible that some of the letters are meant to go together, but they don't form any recognizable word.

C. *Lines, pictures, or letters are randomly placed on the page.*

This piece might be viewed from several sides. Without help from the writer, it's hard to determine where to start looking on the page.

D. *Lines, pictures, or letters are grouped haphazardly.*

Some lines may be part of a letter or part of a picture.

E. *There is no sense of order.*

It's almost impossible to know where to look first. The placement of the picture and letters does not appear to be connected.

What We Say to the Writer

It looks like there are three parts to your paper, and that you may be trying to organize your piece with a beginning, a middle, and an ending. Can you show me where to start? What happens next? How does your piece end? It helps me understand your message when you organize your work like that.

Ideas

Organization

Voice

Word Choice

Sentence Fluency

Conventions

Analysis of the Organization Trait in "Savanna"

What We See in the Writing

Clearly, there is a strong sense of organization in this piece. Circles containing words or names are connected by lines. There are three such strands. Perhaps this student's teacher has modeled using a graphic organizer. Without the writer's translation, however, it's impossible to determine the meaning or the writer's thinking about why he or she organized the paper this way. This scores at a level 2, Exploring, for the trait of organization.

Scoring Guide

The paper rated these scores on a 5-point scale.

Ideas	1
ORGANIZATION	**2**
Voice	1
Word Choice	1
Sentence Fluency	1
Conventions	1

A. *The piece has no title.*

There is no evidence of a title for this writing.

B. *Letters or words are used as captions.*

This is a tough call. Without clarity from the writer, it's hard to tell whether the words provide some sort of caption for the circles or what the circles represent.

C. *Simple clues about order emerge in pictures or text.*

It appears that the writer uses some sense of organization, as the page has circles that are connected by lines. Each circle contains a name or word.

D. *The arrangement of pictures or text shows an awareness of the importance of structure and pattern.*

The writer organizes words on three separate strands. A literal connection is shown with lines. It's unclear, however, why these words go together.

E. *Left-to-right, top-to-bottom orientation is evident.*

There is evidence of orientation. When holding the paper horizontally, it appears that there is a left-to-right, top-to-bottom orientation. When held vertically, only a top-to-bottom orientation is clear.

F. *No transitions are indicated.*

Words are connected by lines. It's unclear how each word or strand is related to the other.

What We Say to the Writer

I can tell that you're trying to organize your writing by linking words together. How did you decide what order to put them in? Is there a way you might show your reader what comes first, next, then last? You're off to a good start.

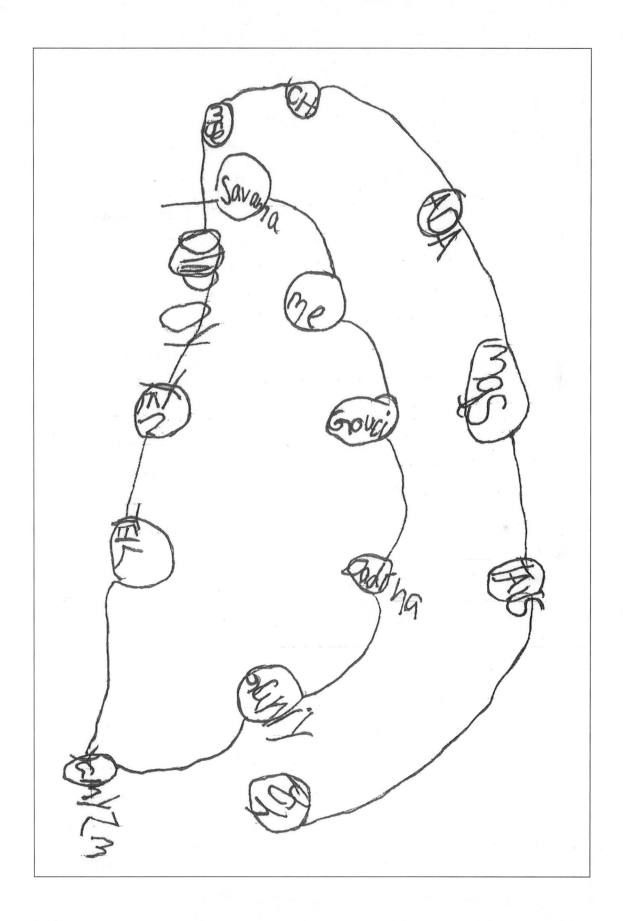

Organization

Ideas

Voice

Word Choice

Sentence Fluency

Conventions

Analysis of the Organization Trait in "We candle fore egg"

What We See in the Writing

The writer is describing what happened when he or she candled eggs to see if the chick inside might move. Exciting stuff! The writer explains what was done, how, and the result, showing that a lot of information can be shared in a short amount of space. Although there are no pictures, the writer is clear and that's what matters most. (In case you are stumped, "BluDwesis" is *blood veins*.)

A. The simple title (if present) states the topic.

The piece does not have a title. An interesting question for this writing might be, "What title should be put on this piece to make sure readers know the idea you are writing about?"

B. The piece contains a beginning but not a conclusion.

There is a sense of beginning as the writer tells us what took place, "we candle fore egg." There is no ending, however. The writer ends after the most exciting part, watching the chick move. This is important to note when talking with the writer because most strong endings come shortly after the high point. The writer could be prompted to tell an ending that would wrap up the experience.

> ### Scoring Guide
> *The paper rated these scores on a 5-point scale.*
>
> | | |
> |---|---|
> | Ideas | 4 |
> | **ORGANIZATION** | **3** |
> | Voice | 2 |
> | Word Choice | 4 |
> | Sentence Fluency | 4 |
> | Conventions | 2 |

C. The piece is little more than a list of sentences connected by a theme.

"We candle fore egg." "We watch BluDwesis" and "Wotch the chick moovieg." These are three distinct events about the science experiment.

D. There is basic order with a few missteps.

The piece is written in a logical order. Moving the information around would confuse the reader, so the writer has used organization even without the traditional transition or sequence words.

E. There is more text at the beginning than in the middle or end.

There was a lot more this writer could have included, but he or she gave us the key information. It's short, but the piece is not weighted too heavily at the beginning or the ending.

F. Sentence parts are linked with conjunctions (but, and, or).

There is one conjunction, *and*, that connects the two activities that take place during the experiment, 1) watch BluDwesls, 2) Wotch the chick moovieg.

What We Say to the Writer

You've done a fine job explaining what happened when we candled the chick eggs today. I like how you told me what you we did first, candling the eggs. Then you explained that you watched the blood veins and saw the chick move. That was exciting, wasn't it? You used a good word here, "and," to connect these two ideas. That's good work in organization! Now, let's think about something you could say right off the bat that would get the reader excited. A piece like this should start off in a fun way.

we candle fore egg
we wotch BluDwesls
and we Wotch the
chick moovieg

Organization

Ideas

Voice

Word Choice

Sentence Fluency

Conventions

Analysis of the Organization Trait in "My frniend"

What We See in the Writing

This writing is organized, with a clear beginning, middle, and end. The text and pictures follow a logical sequence. The writer goes to his friend's house, they play, and, finally, they go outside. Lines visually organize the piece as well. A simple piece, yet well organized for an early first-grade writer. This piece scores a 4, Extending, for organization.

Scoring Guide

The paper rated these scores on a 5-point scale.

Ideas	4
ORGANIZATION	**4**
Voice	3
Word Choice	3
Sentence Fluency	3
Conventions	3

A. The title (if present) comes close to capturing the central idea.

A simple title, "My frniend," lets us know that we'll learn something about the writer's friend.

B. The writing starts out strong but ends predictably.

This writing has a simple yet strong beginning. Each sentence connects easily and leads to a predictable ending.

C. The writer uses a pattern to spotlight the most important details.

The writer visually organizes his writing in segments, separated by lines. Illustrations match the text and are organized using the same format.

D. Ideas follow a logical but obvious sequence.

Going to a friend's house, playing, going outside—it makes perfect sense.

E. The pace of the writing is even; it doesn't bog the reader down.

Clean, simple statements lead to a sensible conclusion: "and we went outside."

F. Basic transitions link one sentence to the next.

This writer includes a conjunction (*and*) to link his last two sentences. The organization of text with matching pictures guides the reader from one sentence or section to the next.

What We Say to the Writer

The way you organized your writing by separating parts with lines works very well. How did you decide to organize it that way? You made it easy for your readers to follow along, and your writing makes sense.

Ideas

Organization

Voice

Word Choice

Sentence Fluency

Conventions

Analysis of the Organization Trait in "A Scary Story"

What We See in the Writing

"A Scary Story" is a pleasure to read. It includes a bold beginning, a mighty middle, and an excellent ending. This piece is well organized and receives a score of 5, Established.

A. *The title (if present) is thoughtful and effective.*

The title, "A Scary Story," is all that's needed to get the reader's attention.

B. *There is a clear beginning, middle, and end.*

There is no clearer beginning than "Once upon a time . . ." The piece moves on to tell us how the vampire spooks several characters. It concludes with a warning to the reader that ". . . he might come for you!!!"

C. *Important ideas are highlighted within the text.*

We know that there's a spooky vampire out there. The writer leads us through several pages of spooking, and then leaves us wondering who will be next. Hmmm . . . sounds like there might be a sequel. Don't all good vampire stories have sequels???

D. *Everything fits together nicely.*

From beginning to end, the writer stays true to the main idea. Using variations of the word "spook" throughout helps tie the pages together.

E. *The text slows down and speeds up to highlight the ideas and shows the writer's skill at pacing.*

The theme begins at a comfortable pace and builds steam as the story ends.

F. *Clear transitions connect one sentence to the next.*

"One night," "Next," "Last," and "Later" link each sentence and page of the story. Concluding with a warning is an excellent ending that will leave the reader sleeping with one eye open.

> ## Scoring Guide
> *The paper rated these scores on a 5-point scale.*
>
> | | |
> |---|---|
> | Ideas | 5 |
> | **ORGANIZATION** | **5** |
> | Voice | 5 |
> | Word Choice | 4 |
> | Sentence Fluency | 5 |
> | Conventions | 4 |

What We Say to the Writer

Your story is well organized and includes a bold beginning, a mighty middle and an excellent ending. It starts out like many fairy tales, with the words "Once upon a time . . . ." Do you like to read fairy tales? You also used words like "next" and "last," which made your story easy to read and understand. I especially liked the ending because it took me by surprise.

A Scary Story

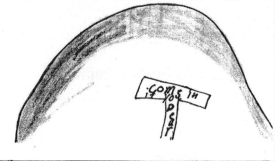

Once upon a time there lived a spooky Vampire. Every night he Wood come out and spook People!

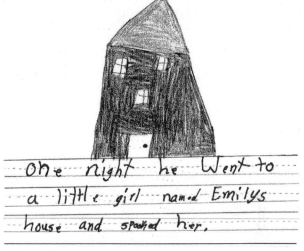

One night he Went to a little girl named Emilys house and spooked her.

Next he spooked a old man in his rocking chair.

Last he gave his Wife a spook.

Later on he Went to bed Youed better Watch out he might come for you!!!

the End

Analysis of the Voice Trait in "I tgr"

What We See in the Writing

The writer's voice just doesn't come through in this piece. There is no feeling of energy in either the text or the illustration. This writing receives a score of 1 for the trait of voice, Ready to Begin.

Scoring Guide

The paper rated these scores on a 5-point scale.

Ideas	1
Organization	1
VOICE	**1**
Word Choice	1
Sentence Fluency	1
Conventions	1

A. *The reader is not sure why the writer chose this idea for writing.*

It's hard to determine what the writer wants us to know. There seems to be a glimmer of an idea here, but the reader needs the help of the writer to understand what it might be.

B. *The writer copies what he or she sees displayed around the room.*

It seems that this writer has focused on dotted letters that are used to teach letter formation. There may be something unique behind those dotted and traced letters, but the writer isn't able to clearly express it yet.

C. *No awareness of audience is evident.*

The writer shows no indication of knowing what the reader will need in order to make sense of this writing.

D. *The piece contains very simple drawings or lines.*

The dotted letters *t, g,* and *r* are clear. The other lines leave questions for the reader: is it the letter *m*? A mountain? Something else? How does it connect to the piece?

E. *Nothing distinguishes the work to make it the writer's own.*

There is nothing here—yet—to show the uniqueness of this writer.

What We Say to the Writer

It looks like you are tracing letters to make a word. Tell me more about that. I wonder if your writing gives your reader a clue about something you like or something you don't like. What do you think? When you let your reader know how you feel about a topic, that's your voice.

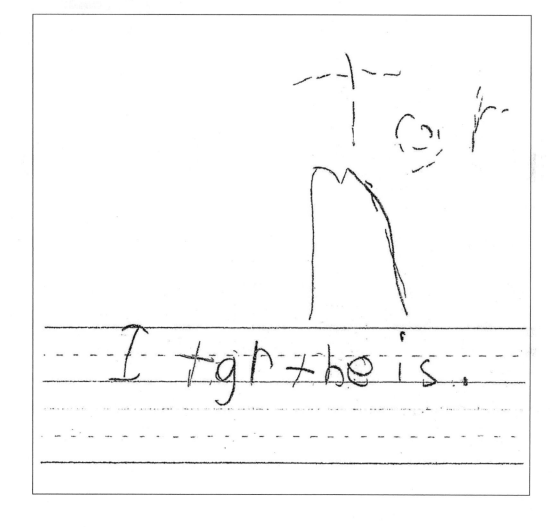

Analysis of the Voice Trait in "This book"

What We See in the Writing

No question how this writer feels about her topic. She loves "et." There's no elaboration as to why she loves *The Kissing Hand*, but her energy certainly shows in her words. The scoring guide descriptors for level 2, Exploring, match this student's writing performance.

A. *The piece is a routine response to the assignment.*

This writer may have been prompted to write about her favorite book. Perhaps she listened to the story and just had to write about it.

B. *The piece is made up of environmental text and only a bit of original text.*

The writer most likely had the book in front of her to copy the title. She added her own original review.

C. *The text connects with the reader in the most general way.*

An enthusiastic statement ("This Book is The GradS Book eavr") connects with the reader.

D. *The drawings begin to reveal the individual.*

This writer knows how to enjoy a good book. A comfy chair (note the plush cushions) plus a good book equals a smiling child, with eyes as big as saucers.

E. *The barest hint of the writer is in evidence.*

The text hints at the sparkle that's still hidden beneath the surface. With more details and elaboration, the writer's voice will shine brightly.

> ### Scoring Guide
> *The paper rated these scores on a 5-point scale.*
>
> Ideas.................................3
> Organization.......................2
> **VOICE** **2**
> Word Choice.......................3
> Sentence Fluency 3
> Conventions.......................2

What We Say to the Writer

I can tell that this must be one of your favorite books. What made it the greatest book ever? When you read The Kissing Hand, *how did it make you feel? When an author makes you feel something as you read a story, that's the trait of voice. Your writing has energy. Writing with energy makes your voice clear for your reader.*

THiS BOOK is THe GrodS BOOK eavr

THe KiSSine Hand

Analysis of the Voice Trait in "My Memory"

What We See in the Writing

This memory piece is focused and connects with readers at a key moment in the text, "a budiful truck" and with the happy driver of the truck smiling out at us. The writer can add more detail and explain how it felt when the truck was crushed or when Mom took it to the dump—either in words or pictures. The beginning is sweet, but the rest of the text simple tells what happens without regard to emotion or reaction by the writer.

A. There are fleeting glimpses of how the writer looks at the topic.

The moment of reflection, "a budiful truck," is endearing.

B. The text and pictures contain touches of originality.

The picture shows a happy driver in good times. This image takes place before the truck gets crushed, of course!

> ### Scoring Guide
> *The paper rated these scores on a 5-point scale.*
>
> | | |
> |---|---|
> | Ideas | 4 |
> | Organization | 4 |
> | **VOICE** | **3** |
> | Word Choice | 3 |
> | Sentence Fluency | 4 |
> | Conventions | 4 |

C. There is a moment of audience awareness, but then it fades.

This truck, this "budiful truck," was important to the writer and though we can assume its demise at the dump was an unhappy experience, it's stated simply without emotion.

D. Oversized letters, exclamation points, underlining, repetition, and pictures are used for emphasis.

The title "MY MEMORY" stands out in this piece. The writer makes a point of letting us know what the piece is about and sets us up for reading.

E. A pat summary statement conceals the writer's individuality.

The piece just ends when the truck does, unceremoniously at the dump.

What We Say to the Writer

You know the part of this piece I love best? It's when you say you had a truck and then you stop and explain that it was a beautiful truck. In that moment I could feel how important that truck was to you. Did you feel anything when the truck was crushed and your mom took it to the dump? What could you write or draw that would help the reader connect with you during that part of your story, too?

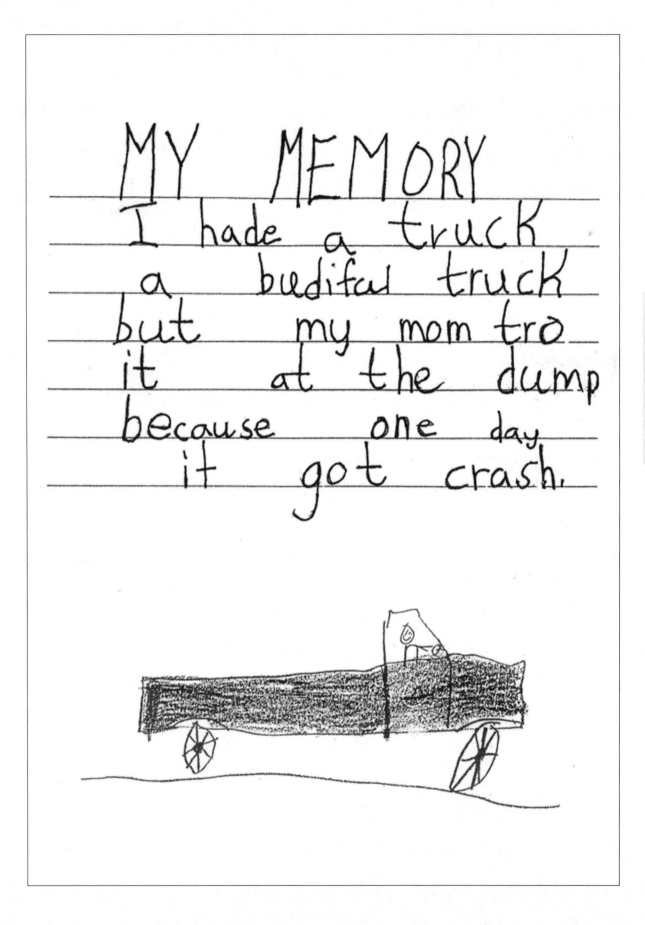

MY MEMORY

I hade a truck
a budiful truck
but my mom tro
it at the dump
because one day
it got crash.

Analysis of the Voice Trait in "DID you KNONOK?"

What We See in the Writing

Oh what fun this writer had candling eggs. It's expressed in the question that draws the reader in. It's expressed in the answer, "Wall ther is!" The writers tells us he or she had fun, but we feel the energy of the piece in the other smooth and natural sounding lines.

A. The writer takes a standard topic and addresses it in a nonstandard way.

The students in the class wrote about their experience candling eggs. This student reached out to the reader by asking a question and drawing the reader into the piece. That's voice!

B. The writer tries a new word, interesting image, or unusual detail.

Trying to intrigue the reader with the concept of a heat lamp, the writer asks if we know about them and assures us they exist.

Scoring Guide

The paper rated these scores on a 5-point scale.

Ideas	3
Organization	4
VOICE	**4**
Word Choice	4
Sentence Fluency	5
Conventions	3

C. The writer speaks to the reader in several places.

A question, "DID You KNONOK that ther is Soting crld a heat lamp?" And the answer, "Walll ther is!" directly addresses the reader and makes a solid connection.

D. The writing captures a general mood, such as happy, sad, or mad.

Without a doubt this writer is excited about the candling experience. So much so, he or she wants us to know something about what was learned: heat lamps.

E. The writer begins to show how he or she really thinks and feels about the topic.

There is much more this writer could say about candling and what happened other than "We had fun." The writer shot off his or her voice cannon in the beginning and lost connection to the reader later in the piece.

What We Say to the Writer

I'd like to hear more about how you used the heat lamp while you candled the eggs. How does a heat lamp work? Can you draw a picture of it or explain it in words? I'm really glad you had fun doing this science experiment. What do you remember most about what you saw? Were you surprised? Nervous? Energized? What words could you use or what pictures could you draw to show how you felt after you got started, all the way to the end of the candling experiment?

DID You KNONOK
taht ther is
sotine crld a
heat lampr walll
ther ist todax
we conldd eggs
We had a fun
the end

Analysis of the Voice Trait in "I'm a fuzzy brown bat"

What We See in the Writing

This writer uses a humorous voice to write about bats. She shares facts in a way that makes the reading pleasurable. There's an overall sense of delight in reading this piece that comes across as energy. "Ah ha!" and "Yes, I'm Safe, Safe, Safe, Safe" are places that reach out and grab the reader's attention. This writing scores as a strong 5, Established, for the voice trait.

A. The writer "owns" the topic.

This writer has done some research on bats. Instead of sharing information in a report format, she writes from the perspective of the bat, which in turn shows how much she understands.

B. The piece contains the writer's imprint.

From beginning to end, this writer uses details to create interesting images. Flying ". . . when the moon is high in the sky" and being "Safe, Safe, Safe, Safe" offer a unique insight into the life of a bat. It's a piece that unmistakably belongs to this writer and this writer alone.

> ### Scoring Guide
> *The paper rated these scores on a 5-point scale.*
>
> | | |
> |---|---|
> | Ideas | 5 |
> | Organization | 5 |
> | **VOICE** | **5** |
> | Word Choice | 5 |
> | Sentence Fluency | 5 |
> | Conventions | 4 |

C. The writer is mindful of his or her audience and connects purposefully to the reader.

"Ah ha! . . . Yes! I caught it! Yummy!" and the ending, "Now it's time for bed. Yawn!" seem guaranteed to put a smile on the reader's face.

D. The tone is identifiable—bittersweet, compassionate, frustrated, terrified, and so on.

The shift in point of view makes this an easy read for voice. It's delightful, energetic, and fun. She's taken a fuzzy brown bat and captured its feelings in a way that young children do best.

E. The writer takes real risks, creating a truly individual piece of writing.

Writing as the bat is a risk that pays off for this writer. Clearly, the writer has put thought into writing about bats in a memorable way. Most likely, she and her audience will remember these facts about bats for a long time to come.

What We Say to the Writer

I would never have thought about sharing information this way. Your voice really comes through when you use your sense of humor to bring out the ideas. I think that you and your classmates will remember the information you shared about bats for a long, long time. I can't wait to read your next voice-filled piece.

I'm a fuzzy brown bat.
I fly only at night when the moon
is high in the sky Ah ha! I spootted
a Juicy looking firefly. Yes! I caught it!
Yummy! Oh NO! There is a owl! It
spotted me! I must get home for the
sun is rising and I'm beeing chaced!
Yes, I'm Safe, Safe, Safe, Safe.
Now It's time for bed. Yawn!

Analysis of the Word Choice Trait in "Playdrama"

Assessment: What We See in the Writing

This young writer expresses much through her drawings. The words may be a label of sorts, perhaps something to do with the drama corner in her classroom. The reader needs help from the writer in order to understand the message. This piece scores a 1, Ready to Begin, for the trait of word choice.

Scoring Guide

The paper rated these scores on a 5-point scale.

Ideas	2
Organization	2
Voice	2
WORD CHOICE	**1**
Sentence Fluency	1
Conventions	1

A. The page contains scribbles and random lines.

Letters and pictures make up this piece.

B. Imitation letters may be present.

Recognizable letters are present. Some letters have been formed incorrectly.

C. There may be random strings of letters across the page.

Letters string across the page and appear to trail off in the middle of the string.

D. Writer uses his or her name.

There is no evidence of the writer's name. The drawing seems to be the focus, and it's possible that the writer was intent on getting that part done first, thus forgetting to write her name.

E. Few, if any, recognizable words are present.

Hard to tell for sure, but the first part of the writing may read "PlaY Drama." Without the writer's help, that's a guess, at best.

What We Say to the Writer

Your picture looks like lots of friends playing. I can see that you wrote the word play, *too. Writers use words to paint a picture in their readers' minds. That's the trait of word choice. You painted a picture with your drawing and words. What a great start.*

Ideas

Organization

Voice

Word Choice

Sentence Fluency

Conventions

Analysis of the Word Choice Trait in "October the 18 8"

What We See in the Writing

A quick glance at this paper shows lots of letters strung together. There's more than meets the eye, however, when you take a closer look. The message that the writer is going to a skating rink becomes quite obvious. A little spacing, and this piece would score higher. The scoring guide descriptors for level 2, Exploring, match this writer's performance.

A. Conventional letters are present.

Letters are present and recognizable in this writing.

B. The letter strings begin to form words.

The letters are grouped in a logical way.

Scoring Guide

The paper rated these scores on a 5-point scale.

Ideas	2
Organization	2
Voice	2
WORD CHOICE	**2**
Sentence Fluency	2
Conventions	1

C. Letter strings can be read as words even though the spacing and spelling aren't correct.

Though letters are strung together, the experienced reader gets the gist of the message: Mom is taking the writer to a skating rink.

D. Words from the board, displays, or word walls are attempted.

This writer most likely copied the date from the board or a morning message. Other words may have come from a word wall or personal spelling list.

E. A few words can be identified.

Several recognizable words can be picked out of the string of letters. *I, am, go, to, skating, rink, mom,* and *you* are quite clear. The date, "October the18," is also easily read. Other words need interpretation. It would seem reasonable that the teacher or a print-rich environment supplied some of the words used in this piece.

What We Say to the Writer

I can tell that you must love going to the skating rink. In your picture, you look happy to be going. Can you tell me your favorite word that describes something about the skating rink or skating? I'll write it on a sticky note for you. That will be a good word choice for you to use to paint a picture with words for your reader the next time you write about skating.

October the 18   8

I am gow go to ha waskati hgrihk
momtakyou

Analysis of the Word Choice Trait in "My mom had sergury"

What We See in the Writing

This writer paints a picture of his mom's knee following surgery. My guess is that his observations have created a new list of words ("sergury," "hols," "cask," "scab") that he can have fun with in his writing . . . at least for a while. This piece receives a score of 3, Expanding, for the trait of word choice.

A. Some words make sense.

Word choice for this piece is clear and makes sense.

B. The reader begins to see what the writer is describing.

The writer "graphically" describes Mom's recovery from surgery. His description of two holes in her knee and Mom peeling the scab off are details that paint a clear picture for the reader.

C. One or two words stand out.

Certainly, "serguy" is not an everyday word. The writer also chooses "beter" over the easier-to-use—and spell—word *good*.

D. Occasional misuse of words bogs the reader down.

The writer does a fine job with word choice. The writing is easy to read and understand.

E. The writer tries out new words.

This piece has a number of words that were a stretch for a young writer: "serguy," "hols in her nee," "cask" (for *cast*), "peling." The writer uses them well, and his voice peeks through when he writes that it looks cool when Mom peels her scab off.

Scoring Guide

The paper rated these scores on a 5-point scale.

Ideas	4
Organization	4
Voice	3
WORD CHOICE	**3**
Sentence Fluency	3
Conventions	3

What We Say to the Writer

When I read your writing, I could picture your mom's knee. Did you use any words that were new for you when you wrote this? Do you have a favorite word in this piece? Your word choice is very precise, and it makes your writing interesting to read.

My mom had sergury a long time ago. She is filing beter. She has just tow hols in her nee. It looks beter. She has her cask off. She is peling ti scab off. It looks cool.

Analysis of the Word Choice Trait in "Catherine's Snowgirl"

Assessment: What We See in the Writing

Some clear and precise words are used in this whimsical story. If there is a snowman, then it stands to reason that there must be a snowgirl. This writing scores a 4, Extending, for the trait of word choice.

A. Proper nouns (e.g., Raisin Bran) are combined with generic ones (e.g., cereal).

Snowgirl and *snowpeople* are more descriptive than using only the more common *snowman*.

B. The writer uses an active verb or two.

Invited, kicked off, and *danced* add variety and energy to this writing.

C. There is very little repetition of words.

Though there is some repetition of *snowpeople* (or a variation of it), it works. The writer uses a variety of other words, and there is less repetition at the end.

D. The writer attempts figurative language.

The writer has used personification well in this story. With more exposure, it won't be long before this writer begins to experiment with metaphors and similes in her writing. The story of a snowgirl making her mate out of snow and ending with the writer knowing ". . . that they must have done something last night" creates an image in the reader's mind.

E. The writer "stretches" by using different types of words.

The writer has made "just right" choices for her topic. Not necessarily showy words, but ones that paint a picture of the night two snowpeople got married.

> ### Scoring Guide
> *The paper rated these scores on a 5-point scale.*
>
> Ideas................................5
> Organization.........................5
> Voice................................5
> **WORD CHOICE**.......................**4**
> Sentence Fluency.....................5
> Conventions..........................4

What We Say to the Writer

When you used verbs like kicked *and* danced*, it really painted a clear picture of your story in my mind. How did you decide to use the word* snowgirl *in your story? That was a great word choice. Close your eyes now and picture your snowgirl. Can you think of one or two words that describe your snowgirl and give her more sparkle? I'll write down what you say on a sticky note.*

Catherine's Snowgirl

Guess what my snowgirl did last night. My snowgirl took more snow and made a snowman. They got married.

They invited other snowmen and snowgirls. My snowgirl kicked off her shoes and danced until midnight. Then they ate cake. At four o clock all the snowpeople went home. The next morning I woke up. When I looked out my window I saw two snowpeople.

I knew that they must have done something last night. I think they're in love.
        the end.

Analysis of the Word Choice Trait in "I like 2nd grade"

What We See in the Writing

This is a piece that sparkles with word choice and voice. I'm sure this writer's teacher smiled as she read that her dad ". . . is a jeanyus he helped me make a RooF yanow." On top of that, the gingerbread houses were "delish." People at the Food Network would probably get a kick out of reading this, too. The scoring guide descriptors for level 5, Established, match this writer's performance.

Scoring Guide

The paper rated these scores on a 5-point scale.

Ideas	5
Organization	4
Voice	5
WORD CHOICE	**5**
Sentence Fluency	4
Conventions	3

A. The writer uses everyday words and phrases with a fresh and original spin.

Phrases such as "remember when" and "by the way" add energy in this writing.

B. The words paint a clear picture in the reader's mind.

Why is 2nd grade better? The writer paints a clear picture of a standout experience that made a difference to him.

C. The writer uses just the right words or phrases.

Clever words and phrases are used from start to finish. "Plus were did you get the idda." I'm sure his teacher smiles every time she reads this piece.

D. The piece contains good use of figurative language.

There is no evidence of figurative language. However, the deliberate word choices add sparkle and life to the writing. My guess is that with more exposure and modeling, this writer will incorporate figurative language in his writing soon.

E. Words are used correctly, colorfully, and with creativity.

"By the way your dad is a jeanyus he helped me make a RooF yanow. Also they were delish." Colorful and spirited words show the reader just why 2nd grade is better.

What We Say to the Writer

Your writing sparkles and your voice shines through. I love the way you used the word genius. *I think that's a splendid word. I also like the word* delish—*it tickles my tongue. How would you describe that word? (Tasty word, food word, fun word, other . . .) Wouldn't it be fun to add more new words to that category and try using them in your writing?*

I like 2nd grade better becuase we made the ginger bread houses. Remember when your Mom and dad came in. By the way your dad is a jeanyhs he helped me make a Roof. yanow. Also they were delish. Plus were did you get the idda. 2nd grade is so Fun!

Ideas

Organization

Voice

Word Choice

Sentence Fluency

Conventions

Analysis of the Sentence Fluency Trait in "Untitled"

What We See in the Writing

Without a title, text, or clear picture, it's hard to tell what this story is about. There may be some awareness of a left-to-right progression on the page. This piece scores at level 1, Ready to Begin, in sentence fluency.

A. *It is hard to figure out connections between text elements.*

There appear to be two parts to this piece. How they go together is the big question.

B. *Words, if present, stand alone.*

No words are present, nor is there a name. What could be a backwards letter *J* is at the top of the page. It's unclear whether that represents the writer's name, a word, or part of the illustration.

> ### Scoring Guide
> *The paper rated these scores on a 5-point scale.*
>
> | | |
> |---|---|
> | Ideas | 1 |
> | Organization | 1 |
> | Voice | 1 |
> | Word Choice | 1 |
> | **SENTENCE FLUENCY** | **1** |
> | Conventions | 1 |

C. *Imitation words and letters are used across the page.*

Lines, the possible backwards *J* . . . they're part of this story. Without text and/or an interpretation from the writer, it's impossible to determine what the message is.

D. *There is no overall sense of flow to the piece.*

There is no real flow to give a sense of fluency to this piece. The sharp angles of some of the lines actually make it feel even less fluent.

E. *Only the writer can read the piece aloud.*

The writer's interpretation is definitely needed for this one. Even the topic can't be determined without the writer's help.

What We Say to the Writer

It looks like you're moving across the page from left to right. That's just how it works when we write a sentence on a page. It's also one of the first steps in becoming a fluent writer.

Analysis of the Sentence Fluency Trait in "Only a Kid"

What We See in the Writing

This writer has grouped words together in what appears to be a list. The clean separation of these groups of words forms an awareness of sentences as thoughts. Though the reader doesn't know what this piece says, each line does begin differently. For sentence fluency, this scores a level 2, Exploring.

Scoring Guide

The paper rated these scores on a 5-point scale.

Ideas	2
Organization	2
Voice	1
Word Choice	2
SENTENCE FLUENCY	**2**
Conventions	1

A. *Words and punctuation marks work together in units.*

Sentences are not present, but words and letters are grouped into a sentence-like formation.

B. *The piece contains many short, repetitive phrases.*

It appears that the writing is made up of short phrases, though they are not repetitive.

C. *Awkward language patterns break the flow of the piece.*

The first and last lines are difficult to decipher. At the end, it seems that the writer is losing stamina. The letters turn into squiggles. The middle two lines appear to say "play outside" and "watch tv." These phrases don't necessarily add to the flow of the writing.

D. *The reader gets only one or two clues about the connection between pictures and text.*

Since no picture is present, it's impossible to determine whether the writer would have clearly connected a picture with the text. It just may be that a picture would have helped the reader understand the message of the writing.

E. *The writer stumbles when reading the text aloud and may have to back up and reread.*

This would probably be difficult for the writer to read aloud. Without spaces between "words," or a picture to jog his memory, the writer might need to make it up as he goes along.

What We Say to the Writer

Is this a list of things that only a kid can do? I noticed that you separated each thing on your list, and you used different words to start each line of your list. You also had some longer lines and some shorter lines. Those are exactly the things that writers do to make their writing sound fluent.

Ideas

Organization

Voice

Word Choice

Sentence Fluency

Conventions

OnIyakid
Kootay hrsfono
playoots
Wooht vs
LeLs to redoi pas h g

Analysis of the Sentence Fluency Trait in "Dr. Martin L. King, Jr."

What We See in the Writing

This writer has done some research. There's lots of information here, but the piece does not read as fluently as it could. The writer will be on his way once he becomes more adept at varying sentence lengths and sentence beginnings. The scoring guide descriptors for level 3, Expanding, match this writer's performance for the trait of sentence fluency.

Scoring Guide

The paper rated these scores on a 5-point scale.

Ideas 5

Organization 4

Voice 3

Word Choice 3

SENTENCE FLUENCY **3**

Conventions 4

A. *Simple sentences contain basic subject-verb agreement (e.g., "I jump").*

Subject-verb agreement is present.

B. *Sentence beginnings are structured identically, making all sentences sound alike.*

Six of eight sentences begin with "He." The other two are back-to-back and begin almost the same way ("Blacks," "Black"), making the sentences sound very similar.

C. *Longer sentences go on and on.*

The longer sentences are a good length. The writing will flow more smoothly as the writer learns to mix shorter and longer sentences.

D. *Simple conjunctions such as* and *and* but *are used to make compound sentences.*

The writer has not attempted to make compound sentences using simple conjunctions.

E. *The piece is easy to read aloud, although it may contain repetitive or awkward sentence patterns.*

The writer is knowledgeable about the topic. The piece is choppy when read aloud. There is a glimpse of better fluency in the two longer sentences.

What We Say to the Writer

Your piece has so much information about Dr. Martin Luther King, Jr., in it. You must have done some research before you started writing. I notice that a lot of your sentences begin with the word he. *If you connect some of the sentences with words like* and *or* but, *and start your sentences with different words, it will make your writing more fluent. When writing is fluent, it sounds smoother and is easier to read. Let's see where we might make some changes like that. We'll look at it together.*

Dr. Martin L. King, Jr.
He was born on January 15, 1929.
He brought peace to people.
He was a prea cher.
He helped change laws. Blacks could not drink from the same water fountain an whites. Black and white people could not go to the same school. He helped changed this. He was killed in 1968.

Ideas

Organization

Voice

Word Choice

Sentence Fluency

Conventions

Analysis of the Sentence Fluency Trait in "I admire my brother"

What We See in the Writing

In "I admire my brother" the writer is capturing the essence of the sentence fluency trait. The piece is short but fluent. Fluency improves as the piece moves from beginning to end. The descriptors for level 4, Extending, match this writing.

A. Sentences are of different lengths.

Sentence length varies from beginning to end. The first few sentences are rather short, but the piece ends with more complex sentences. This adds to the overall flow of the writing.

B. Sentences start differently.

Though many of the sentences begin with "He," it doesn't bog the piece down because of the varying sentence lengths.

C. Some sentences read smoothly, while others still need work.

The cluster of shorter sentences at the beginning would benefit from some revision. The writer becomes more fluent at the end of the piece.

D. Conjunctions are correctly used in long and short sentences.

The writer stays connected to the topic, his brother, throughout the writing.

E. Aside from a couple of awkward moments, the piece can be read aloud easily.

This piece can be read aloud easily. The writer has good control of conventions, which contributes to fluency.

What We Say to the Writer

When I read your piece, it flows smoothly and fluently. Even though you start several sentences with "He is . . .," I still feel a nice rhythm in your writing. By mixing in the word also ("He is also a good reader"), and creating a more complex sentence at the end ("He is always . . ."), you have added fluency to your writing.

Scoring Guide

The paper rated these scores on a 5-point scale.

Ideas	4
Organization	4
Voice	4
Word Choice	4
SENTENCE FLUENCY	**4**
Conventions	4

I admire my brother, Ashton! He is a good drawer. He is also a good reader. Ashton likes to swing. He has a bunch of stuffed animals that he plays with all the time. He is always there for me when I need him!

Analysis of the Sentence Fluency Trait in "Dec. 26th"

What We See in the Writing

This first-grade writer provides an example of fluent writing in a content area. The ending illustrates how voice can also play a role in content-area writing. This piece receives a score of 5, Established, for the trait of sentence fluency.

A. Different sentence lengths give the writing a nice sound. There is playfulness and experimentation.

This writer has struck a nice balance in this writing by varying sentence length. The voice and heart of this young writer are evident in the writing on this important topic.

B. Varied sentence beginnings create a pleasing rhythm.

"Dec. 26th . . .," "over 600 people . . .," "So far . . .," "So maby . . . " create a rhythm and flow that please the reader.

> ## Scoring Guide
> *The paper rated these scores on a 5-point scale.*
>
> | | |
> |---|---|
> | Ideas | 4 |
> | Organization | 5 |
> | Voice | 5 |
> | Word Choice | 4 |
> | **SENTENCE FLUENCY** | **5** |
> | Conventions | 4 |

C. Different kinds of sentences (statements, commands, questions, and exclamations) are present.

This content-area piece is made up of statements, and ends with a plea.

D. The flow from one sentence to the next is smooth.

Sentences flow smoothly from one to the next. Though *so* seems to be a favorite starter word for this writer, in time it will be replaced with more appropriate variations. For now, it works in this piece.

E. The piece is a breeze to read aloud.

This writing is easy to read aloud. The writer's compassion comes through loud and clear. There is almost a crescendo building up to the final sentence: "So please lets help them."

What We Say to the Writer

I loved reading your piece out loud. You started some of your sentences with words or phrases that are different from the way sentences often begin. That makes your writing fluent to read. Did you read it out loud to hear how fluently the sentences fit together?

Dec. 26th there was a Tsunami. over 600 people are trying to help. So far the School has collected $400.97. So maby the whole world can help. We could give them food, water, clothes. or even a home. We could mail them a letter to make them feel better. So please let's help Them.

Ideas

Organization

Voice

Word Choice

Sentence Fluency

Conventions

Analysis of the Conventions Trait in "rskyler"

What We See in the Writing

This young writer is using pictures as the main means to communicate in this piece. The pictures are detailed, a good start for a beginning writer. Therefore, this paper receives a score of 1, Ready to Begin, for the trait of conventions.

A. Letters are written in strings (pre-phonetic spelling, such as GmkrRt).

An experienced reader might pick out the word *sky* in this writing. It's hard to tell if that's intentional or just a bit of luck in this string of letters.

B. Letters are formed irregularly; there is no intentional use of uppercase and lowercase letters.

This piece has a combination of uppercase and lowercase letters. In some cases, the letters look more like squiggles.

C. Spacing is uneven between letters and words.

While there is no evidence of spacing between letters or words, it's possible that the very beginnings of such knowledge are present in the illustration.

D. Punctuation is not present.

This student is working hard to get some letters on the paper. Punctuation will just have to wait.

E. The piece does not contain standard conventions.

There is no evidence, yet, of standard writing conventions.

> ## Scoring Guide
>
> *The paper rated these scores on a 5-point scale.*
>
> Ideas 1
> Organization 2
> Voice 1
> Word Choice 1
> Sentence Fluency 1
> **CONVENTIONS** **1**

What We Say to the Writer

When I look at your writing, I see letters that you've written on the lines, and I see lots of details in your picture. This looks like the word sky. Are you telling about the clouds in the sky? I love that you left some spaces between your pictures. If you leave spaces between your words, too, it will make your writing easier to read.

Analysis of the Conventions Trait in "Theis hat macks"

What We See in the Writing

The memory that a hat evokes for this child creates a piece that is strong for the trait of ideas. It looks like our writer is holding onto some of the things he hears from his teacher—in this case, to put a period at the end of the sentence. The difference between placing the period at the end of a line versus the end of a sentence is one of the things this student is still figuring out. This paper scores a 2, Exploring, for the trait of conventions.

Scoring Guide

The paper rated these scores on a 5-point scale.

Ideas	4
Organization	3
Voice	3
Word Choice	3
Sentence Fluency	3
CONVENTIONS	**2**

A. *The words are unreadable to the untrained eye (quasi-phonetic spelling, such as KN, sD, Wt).*

While primary teachers will be able to read this piece, most others will have difficulty. Simple words (*hat, me, I, at, my, and, to, by, the*) help connect those that are challenging.

B. *There is little discrimination between uppercase and lowercase letters.*

There is a mix of uppercase and lowercase letters. The writer seems fairly consistent using uppercase (*M, N*) while others are hard to tell because of size (*c, k, s, o*).

C. *Spacing between letters and words is present.*

This student understands the need for spacing between letters and words.

D. *The writer experiments with punctuation.*

Periods are important, and the end of a line (not sentence) seems like a good place for important punctuation. Interestingly, three of the last four lines are not punctuated with a period. And while the writer skipped lines at the beginning, the end was single-spaced. Perhaps this young writer became fatigued.

E. *The use of conventions is not consistent.*

Experimenting with spelling, a liberal sprinkling of periods at the end of most lines, and many uppercase and lowercase letters in the correct place are indications that this writer is on his way to using standard writing conventions.

What We Say to the Writer

I've noticed that you must be remembering how important it is to use periods in writing. Periods show us the end of a complete thought and give us a place to take a breath. I'll read this to you so that you can tell me where to stop at the end of the thought. Then we'll check to see if the periods are in the right place. Note: While there are several teaching points that might be made here, we'll address just one thing at a time.

theis hat Macks.
Me rymamBr win.
I livd at.
Gramos and Grapos.
Me and GraPo.
wint to LPaso to.
gathR we drov by
the brij theat.
saPras LPaso and
MaxicKo

Analysis of the Conventions Trait in "I love my bear"

What We See in the Writing

The conventions in this writing are at the midpoint. The writer is accurately using what she's learned, but is not yet ready to take risks. The scoring guide descriptors for level 3, Expanding, match this writing for the trait of conventions.

Scoring Guide

The paper rated these scores on a 5-point scale.

Ideas	4
Organization	3
Voice	3
Word Choice	3
Sentence Fluency	3
CONVENTIONS	**3**

A. *Spelling is inconsistent but readable (phonetic spelling, such as kitn, sed, wnt).*

Most words are spelled correctly. Others, such as "wene" and "veary," are quite readable.

B. *Uppercase and lowercase letters are used correctly.*

It appears that uppercase and lowercase letters are used correctly. The lines on this writing paper may be challenging for this particular writer. Wider line spacing and a dotted midline might still be beneficial.

C. *Capitals mark the beginnings of sentences.*

Capitals mark the beginning of sentences, with the exception of the last one. The writer has also changed several of her letter *m* formations so that they are now correct for their position in the sentence.

D. *End punctuation marks are generally used correctly.*

All end punctuation (periods) has been used correctly.

E. *The writing follows simple conventions correctly.*

This piece is easy to read. Conventions are simple, but work well.

What We Say to the Writer

Your writing conventions are strong. You've remembered to leave a space between words, use capital letters at the beginning of sentences, and put periods at the end of sentences. That makes it easy for others to read. You also spelled the first syllable of the word very *with the same letters that are in the word* bear. *That's a good idea when you're spelling words that are challenging for you.* Very *is a tricky word to spell. Let me show you how it looks in writing.*

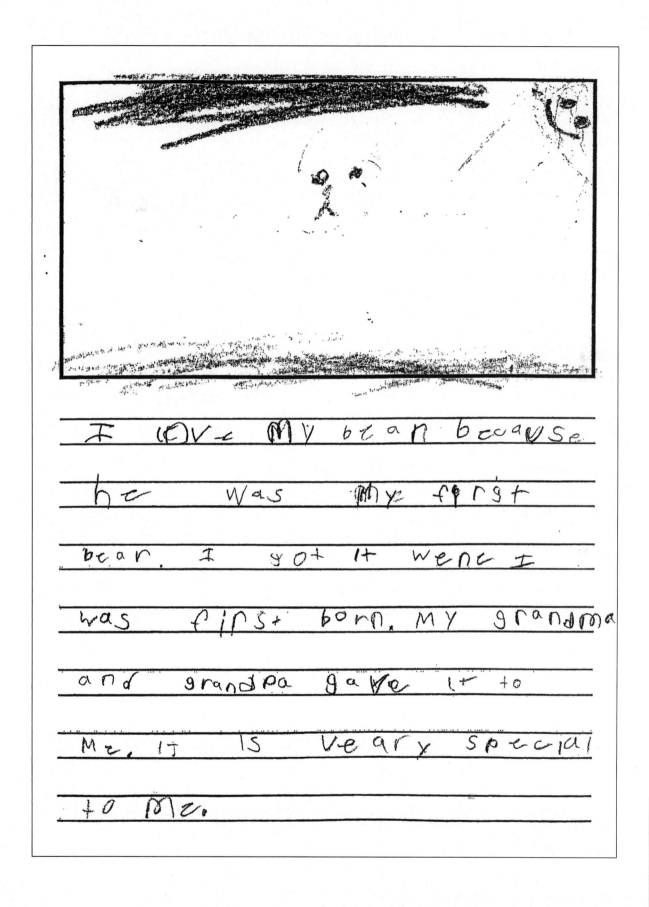

I love my bear because he was my first bear. I got it wenc I was first born. My grandma and grandpa gave it to me. It is veary special to me.

Ideas

Organization

Voice

Word Choice

Sentence Fluency

Conventions

Analysis of the Conventions Trait in "Justin's Crab"

What We See in the Writing

"Justin's Crab" contains correct spelling and use of uppercase and lowercase letters. Punctuation is simple, and the writer has used the possessive form accurately in *Justin's*. Once this writer is ready to take some risks with more advanced punctuation and sophisticated word choice, his writing will score higher. I score this piece as a strong 4, Extending, for the trait of conventions.

> ### Scoring Guide
> *The paper rated these scores on a 5-point scale.*
>
> Ideas 5
> Organization 4
> Voice 3
> Word Choice 4
> Sentence Fluency 4
> **CONVENTIONS** **4**

A. *Spelling is correct or close on high-use words (e.g., kiten, saed, wint).*

High-use and more difficult words (*the, when, scared, night*) are spelled correctly.

B. *Sentence beginnings and proper nouns are usually capitalized.*

Sentence beginnings and proper nouns are all capitalized. Upon closer inspection, we can see that the writer initially began his second sentence with a lowercase *w*. Credit goes to him for remembering to change it to an uppercase letter at the beginning of a sentence.

C. *The writer uses end punctuation and series commas correctly.*

Each sentence ends neatly with a period. No commas have been used, leading the reader to believe that the writer isn't quite ready for that risk yet.

D. *The writer may try more advanced punctuation (dashes, ellipses, quotation marks), but not always with success.*

Apostrophes (in the contraction *I'm* and the possessive *Justin's*) are the only advanced punctuation used.

E. *Only minor editing is required to show thoughtful use of conventions.*

A few well-placed commas would move this to a strong piece in conventions.

What We Say to the Writer

The conventions are strong in your writing. Did you use a dictionary to help you spell more difficult words? I can tell that you reread your piece, as it looks like you changed some uppercase and lowercase letters to what they needed to be. That's what writers do. I would love to see you add some commas to your piece. We can look at that together. I would also encourage you to try using some new punctuation marks to change how the writing sounds. That will help bring out your voice. That's a good next step for you as a writer.

Justin's crab

I'm Justin's crab and when he tris to water my spong-- or feed me I snap at him. When I get scared I tuck into my shell. I dig holes and sleep in them in the night.

Analysis of the Conventions Trait in "Underwater Dragonfly"

What We See in the Writing

This writer has mastered standard conventions. He is now experimenting (remarkably well) with more sophisticated and challenging punctuation and vocabulary. Ending with a question mark spotlights the playful voice of this writer. The scoring guide descriptors for level 5, Established, match this writer's performance for the trait of conventions.

A. High-use words are spelled correctly and others are easy to read.

Not only are all the words in this writing spelled correctly, but some are quite challenging (*swimming, antennae*).

B. The writer applies basic capitalization rules with consistency.

This writer got them all. He's consistent in using uppercase letters at the beginning of each sentence, and he didn't forget to use an uppercase *J* in January—even though it's not the first word in the sentence.

> ### Scoring Guide
> *The paper rated these scores on a 5-point scale.*
>
> Ideas 5
> Organization 5
> Voice 5
> Word Choice 5
> Sentence Fluency 5
> **CONVENTIONS** **5**

C. Punctuation marks are used effectively to guide the reader.

You can tell that this young writer has learned much about different punctuation. From the ellipses to quotation marks to commas and different end punctuation, this writer does it well.

D. One or more indented paragraphs are present.

Though the paragraphs are not indented, the spacing sets them off in a very visual way.

E. Standard English grammar is used.

Grammar usage is correct.

F. Conventions are applied consistently and accurately.

Conventions are accurate, making this piece easy to read and follow.

What We Say to the Writer

You used some different punctuation marks in your writing. How did you decide to try these things? Did you see them in books you've read? I can tell that you're noticing what authors do in their writing to make it interesting for the reader. Often, this highlights the voice trait. Ending with a question brought out your voice. When you try new things in your writing, as you did in this piece, it makes your writing stronger.

Underwater Dragonfly

One January day, a little dragonfly hatched from an egg. He swam faster and faster. And then he...

...to be continued...

No, just joking! Then he said to himself, "I love my fins and my gills!" He thought his antennae were his gills and his wings were his fins.

When years passed, he got bigger but still stayed in the water.

Do you like my story?

Guidelines for Using the Interactive PDFs on the CD

On the enclosed CD, you'll find PDFs of all 30 papers from the book. You can print them or project them on a screen for whole-class discussion, using your whiteboard tools to highlight, comment, even revise and edit.

In addition, you'll find 12 interactive PDFs, a high and low paper for each trait. Navigation buttons at the bottom of each page step you through the four key qualities for the particular trait. For each key quality, we provide a discussion prompt to help students notice what's working well in a paper or what needs more work. You'll also find a final page on which students are prompted to try out a revision or editing strategy on their own writing based on what they learned from the high example.

Here's a sample routine for working with the interactive PDFs:

1. Display the paper from the Interactive PDFs folder.

2. Read the paper aloud to the class. Discuss the drawings and text.

3. Review the corresponding scoring guide. You may display this side-by-side with the paper or have students consult their own copies.

4. Compare the paper to the scoring guide and decide where the paper falls on the continuum. Invite a student to mark on the arrow running alongside the paper about where the class determines the paper should score.

5. Explore one or more key qualities by clicking on the corresponding navigation buttons at the bottom of the page. The highlighted parts indicate words or passages we focused on as we evaluated the paper. Follow the prompts to guide students' exploration of the key quality.

6. Extend the learning by clicking on the "What would make the trait strong?" button (for the low papers) or the "What have learned about the trait?" button (high papers).

CD Contents:

- Scoring Guides (teacher version)
- Student Friendly Scoring Guides (two versions)
- Editor's Marks reference sheet
- PDFs of all student papers
- Guidelines for Using the Interactive PDFs on the CD
- 12 interactive PDFs

> **TIP**
>
> To view and print the files on the CD, you need Adobe Reader™, version 7.0 or higher. You can download it free of charge for Mac and PC systems at www.adobe.com/products/acrobat